The do-it-yourself Guide to...

Mommy Sanity

by

Marianne Richmond

The do-it-yourself Guide to...
Mommy Sanity

Marianne Richmond Studios, Inc.
420 N. 5th Street, Suite 840
Minneapolis, MN 55401
www.mariannerichmond.com

ISBN 0-9753528-4-9

Illustrations by Marianne Richmond

Book design by Sara Dare Biscan

Printed in China

Second Printing

TO

FROM

Date

If you're a mom, you know the deal.
A day can last <u>forever</u>. A year flies by!

Being a mom is the hardest,
most demanding and most adventurous
job you'll ever have. And, the most
rewarding! What occupation can rival
that of raising a human being?

But let's get real. Some days are so
unpredictably challenging, tiring...
and downright annoying that you're
not sure you'll see 'em to eighteen!

Well, girlfriend, <u>cheer</u> up!
   We have created just for you...

The do-it-yourself Guide to...
   (maintaining your) Mommy Sanity
in the hopes of getting you to laugh...
   before you cry.

So, try some of our strategies and
   remember... you are the most
important person in the world to
   however many little people
call you mom!

Hearing the word "Mom"
482 times in one hour.

The endless tidying.

Being cried on,
coughed on,
and thrown up on
once too often.

Their bickering...

and whining.

Your lack of sleep.

...and being too tired
for "that," too.

Out of answers...

in want of advice,

and in serious need
of a vacation.

Guilt.

Even more guilt.

The "should" dinner.

The perfectly acceptable
alternative.

Oh, _and_ the expectation
to anticipate
everyone's needs.

And should you still feel

on the brink?

cherish it!

A gifted author and artist, Marianne Richmond shares
her creations with millions of people worldwide
through her delightful books, cards, and giftware.
In addition to the *Simply Said...* and *Smartly Said...*
gift book series, she has written and illustrated four
additional books: **The Gift of an Angel,
The Gift of a Memory, Hooray for You!** and
The Gifts of Being Grand.

To learn more about Marianne's products, please visit
www.mariannerichmond.com.